GRANDTULLY
PRIMARY SCHOOL

MATERIALS AND PROCESSES

Peter Riley

W
FRANKLIN WATTS
NEW YORK•LONDON•SYDNEY

First published in 1998 by
Franklin Watts
96 Leonard Street, London
EC2A 4RH

Franklin Watts Australia
14 Mars Road
Lane Cove
NSW 2066

Editor: Sarah Snashall
Art director: Robert Walster
Designer: Mo Choy

Picture research: Sue Mennell
Photography: Steve Shott
(unless otherwise credited)
Artwork: Sean Wilkinson

A CIP catalogue record for
this book is available from
the British Library.

ISBN 0 7496 2963 0

Dewey classification 620.1

Printed in Belgium

Picture credits:
Robert Harding p.22m
(Martyn F. Chillmaid)
The Image Bank p.19l
(Nick Pavloff)
Images Colour Library pp. 9b, 17tl,
17tr, 18t, 20 (both), 21tm,
21tr, 27l
Life Science Images p.25t
Ray Muller pp. 2, 19r
Science Photo Library pp. 9t,
24b (Adrienne Hart-Davis), 28b (P.
Nieto, Jerrican), 29l (ITAR-
TASS/European Space Agency), 29r
(Dr. Jeremy Burgess)
Still Pictures p.23t
(Andre Maslennikov),
20tl (Marc Rapillard)
The Stockmarket p. 11b
Tony Stone Images p.5t
(Pal Hermansen)
Telegraph Colour Library p. 28t

CONTENTS

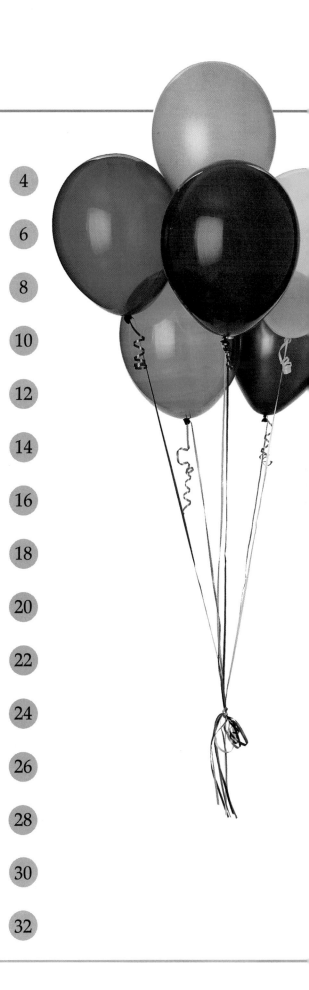

MATERIALS AROUND US

There are thousands of different materials. They are all around us. Clothes are made from wool, cotton and nylon. Homes are made from brick, wood and glass. The Earth is made from rock and the surface of the land is covered with soil and water. Every one of these things – wool, cotton, nylon, brick, wood, glass, rock, soil and water – is a material.

Steel is magnetic. It is attracted to a magnet.

Pottery is brittle. It breaks if it is struck hard.

Cloth is absorbent. It soaks up water.

Plastic is light-weight. It has a small weight for its size.

Water is a solvent. Other substances dissolve in it.

Glass is transparent. Light can pass straight through it.

Stone is heavy. It has a large weight for its size.

Paper is flexible. It bends easily.

PROPERTIES

Materials have properties. A property is a special feature of a material. One property of wood is that wood is hard. One property of wool is that wool is soft. A material can have other properties. It may be strong or weak, flexible or rigid, magnetic or non-magnetic, transparent or opaque.

Wood is flexible. The branches of a tree can bend in the wind.

Brick is rigid. It does not bend.

Wood is opaque. Light cannot pass through it.

Wool is a heat insulator. It does not allow heat to pass through it.

Rubber is elastic. It can be stretched and squashed but returns to its normal size.

The nail does not break when the hammer hits it because it is not brittle. What would happen if the hammer hit the glass?

◼ INVESTIGATE!

List the properties of the materials that make up a window and frame. What materials could have been used instead?

USING MATERIALS

We choose materials to use because they have certain properties. Cotton is soft and this makes it useful for clothing. Glass is transparent and this makes it useful for making windows.

LOTS OF PROPERTIES

Usually it is not just one property of a material which makes it useful, but the combination of its properties. Wood is strong, hard and light in weight.

Each of these properties is useful for making a chair. When you sit on a wooden chair the wood's strength supports your weight and stops the chair from bending. The wood is light enough for you to move the chair easily. Its surface is hard and not easily chipped if it is accidentally knocked.

Metal is harder than wood. It can also be made very thin. This makes it a good material for making a saw.

Rubber is elastic, hard-wearing and grips the road. This makes it suitable for making car tyres.

COMBINING MATERIALS

Many things we use need to have a number of properties. Training shoes have to be light-weight, hard-wearing, springy, firm and sweat-absorbent. No single material has all these properties so a combination of materials is used to make the shoes.

The feet are covered in a moisture absorbing fabric.

The top of the shoes is made from a fabric which allows moisture to pass through it.

The soles are made from rubber which is flexible and hard wearing. The rubber and fabric are held together with strong glue.

INVESTIGATE!

What are the useful properties of cloth in a curtain, rubber in a bicycle tyre and metal in a pair of scissors?

Conducting Heat

Some materials let heat travel through them. They are called conductors of heat. Materials that do not let heat travel through them are called insulators.

Metals and pans

Metals are good conductors of heat. Pans are made of metal because the metal lets heat from the stove pass quickly to the food to cook it.

Central heating

Radiators in a central heating system are made of metal. Hot water moves from the boiler through the pipes to the radiators. The heat in the water passes quickly through the metal in the radiators and out into the air to heat the room.

These clothes are being dried on a central heating radiator because the metal passes heat quickly to them.

STOPPING HEAT MOVING

Some plastics are heat insulators. They are used to make the handles of pans and electric kettles. The surface of the plastic handle stays cool to hold even though the pan or kettle is very hot. Wood is also a heat insulator. Some pan handles are made from wood.

KEEPING WARM

Air is an insulator. Some materials trap air inside them. The air turns the material into an insulator too. Wool fibres are wavy and have air spaces between them. A woollen jumper traps a layer of air over your skin. It stops your body heat escaping and keeps you warm.

The air spaces between the woollen fibres stop heat travelling through the material.

■ INVESTIGATE!

Fill two plastic cups with warm water and wrap a piece of cotton cloth around one cup and a piece of woollen cloth around the other. Which cup of water stays warmer longer? Which material is the better insulator?

This climber is wearing a number of heat insulating layers to keep warm in the cool wind. Air is trapped between each layer.

CONDUCTING ELECTRICITY

Many appliances, such as a television or toaster, need electricity. The electricity flows from a supply of electricity to the appliance through a wire. The wire is a conductor of electricity. It lets the current of electricity flow through it. Most materials do not let electricity flow through them. They are called electrical insulators.

CONDUCTORS

Metals such as iron, steel, copper and aluminium are electrical conductors. The black material in a pencil, called graphite, is not a metal but it conducts electricity. Water also conducts electricity.

INSULATORS

Wood, paper, plastic and bricks are insulators. Air is an insulator too. If it was a conductor, the bulb in the circuit above would light when there was a gap in the circuit.

In the circuit above, the light-bulb is on because the metal spoon in the circuit is an electrical conductor. It would not go on if the spoon was made of wood. A circuit like this one can be used to test materials to find out if they are electrical conductors or electrical insulators.

CONDUCTORS AND INSULATORS IN USE

Conductors and insulators are used to send
electricity safely from one place to another. Electricity
is conducted from plug sockets to appliances by
copper wires coated in plastic. The metal takes the
electricity along the wire and the plastic coating stops
the electricity leaving through the sides when the
wire touches other objects.

*Plugs, leads and
switches are all
covered in plastic to
stop the electricity in
the metal reaching
your fingers.*

*Electricity is conducted from power stations along metal
cables which are held on metal towers called pylons.
Insulating material between the cables and the pylons stops
the electricity flowing down the pylons to the ground.*

■ INVESTIGATE!
• • • • • • • • • • •

Set up the
circuit shown
on page 10.
Test different
materials to
find out which
are conductors
and which are
insulators.

• • • • • • • • • • •

Materials at Home

Every house is made from a large number of materials. Each material has special properties which are used for a particular task. The different materials are used together to make a house.

Plastic is light-weight and easily shaped. It is used to make guttering and pipes that carry water to the drains.

Bricks are strong and do not break up in the rain, wind and frost. They make weather-resistant walls which can support the weight of the roof.

Cement holds the bricks together like glue.

Glass is weather-resistant and transparent. It lets light into the home but keeps out the wind and the rain.

Paint is a mixture of a coloured powder and a liquid. Paint gives a protective coating on wood and stops it soaking up water and rotting.

Roof-tiles are made of baked clay and are weather-resistant.

Rockwool forms a thick blanket which traps air and makes a thick insulation blanket to stop heat escaping through the roof.

Wood is strong yet light in weight and easily shaped. It is used to make the window frames and doors and the roof supports that rest on the walls and hold the roof-tiles.

Electricity is brought to the home by metal cables covered in a coat of insulating material.

Light-weight, opaque fabrics are used to make curtains and heavier, hard-wearing fabrics are used to make carpets and furniture coverings.

Concrete is very strong and hard-wearing. It is used to make the foundations on which the house is built. It may also be used for the ground floor and for the paths outside.

▌INVESTIGATE!

Scratch some pieces of wood, brick, concrete and plastic which are no longer needed. Which material has the hardest surface?

SOLIDS, LIQUIDS AND GASES

Most of the materials around us are solid materials. There are two other types of materials. They are liquids and gases. All materials can be put into one of these three groups – solids, liquids or gases. The materials in each group have properties that are different from the materials in the other two groups.

A SOLID

A solid material has a definite shape and a definite size or volume. It cannot be squashed to fit into a smaller space. Tiny pieces of solids can flow together like the sand in an egg-timer but they do not form drops. Most of the materials around us are solids.

Some solids like these minerals have a crystal shape.

A LIQUID

A liquid does not have a definite shape. It can flow and take up the shape of any container into which it is poured. It also forms drops. A liquid has a definite volume which stays the same even if you try to squash it.

Water is the most common liquid but oil and syrup are liquids too.

A GAS

A gas does not have any definite shape or volume. It fills any container into which it is pushed or poured. The volume can be made smaller by squashing the gas into a small container, or larger by releasing the gas into a large container.

Helium is a gas which is lighter than air and is used to fill party balloons that float upwards.

■ INVESTIGATE!

Different types of liquid flow at different speeds. Prop up a tray to make a shallow slope and trickle different liquids down it such as washing-up-liquid, honey, oil and water. Compare how they run.

SOLID TO LIQUID

Many solid materials turn into liquids when they are heated strongly enough. If they are left to cool down they turn back into solids again.

HOTTING UP

When a solid loses its shape and turns into a liquid we say it has melted. The temperature at which a solid melts is called its melting point. The melting point of ice is 0°C. Solids have different melting points. The melting point of chocolate is 33°C and the melting point of aluminium is 660.5°C.

The heat from a hand is strong enough to melt this chocolate.

COOLING DOWN

When a liquid cools down below its melting point it turns back into a solid. As hot wax runs down the side of a burning candle it becomes cooler and turns back into a solid.

These icicles are dripping because the weather is warm enough to melt them.

The water on this window has frozen because the window is colder than 0°C.

FREEZING

When a liquid material is cooled down, it turns into a solid. If the solid is left to warm up again, it turns back into a liquid. The point at which a liquid turns into a solid is called the freezing point. The freezing point of water is 0°C. At 0°C water turns into ice.

REVERSIBLE CHANGES

When water freezes and becomes ice, it is easy to turn it back into a liquid again by melting it. Freezing is a reversible change – in other words, it can be undone. Reversible changes are always in pairs. One of the changes is the opposite of the other. The opposite of freezing is melting.

■ INVESTIGATE!

Half fill a plastic bottle with water. Draw a line to mark the level of the water. Leave the bottle in the freezer until the water has frozen. What happens to the water level?

LIQUID TO GAS

A liquid can turn into a gas in two ways: by evaporating or by boiling.

EVAPORATION

When water is left uncovered, the water slowly changes into a gas and mixes with the air. This is called evaporation. The gas formed when water evaporates is called water vapour. Wet clothes dry by evaporation when they are hung on a line.

Nearly three-quarters of the Earth is covered by water. Evaporation takes place at its surface and the invisible water vapour mixes with the air.

BOILING

When a liquid is heated strongly enough some of it turns to gas and forms bubbles. They rise to the surface of the liquid and escape into the air. A hot bubbling liquid is called a boiling liquid. The temperature at which a liquid boils is called its boiling point. The boiling point of water is 100°C.

Bubbles of steam rise through the boiling water.

CONDENSATION

Gases change into liquids by condensation. Water vapour is in the air all the time. It condenses when it comes in contact with cold surfaces, like the inside of a window on a cold day. When steam mixes with air it cools below 100°C and turns into clouds of tiny water droplets.

_____*Water droplets*

Steam _____

As steam is cooled down by the air it turns into a cloud of water droplets.

When the air is cold above the surface of the ground, water vapour condenses on the grass and forms dew.

MORE REVERSIBLE CHANGES

Evaporation and condensation are reversible changes. A liquid changes into a gas by evaporation and a gas changes back into a liquid by condensation. Boiling and condensation are reversible changes too.

INVESTIGATE!

Take a cold object like a drinks can from a refrigerator and breathe on it. Look for water condensing on the object.

THE WATER CYCLE

Water travels in a circular path. Water evaporates from the surface of seas and oceans, it travels through the air and through the soil and plants. It falls as rain and returns to the seas and oceans. This path is called the water cycle.

EVAPORATION AND CONDENSATION

At the surface of every ocean, sea and lake, water evaporates into the air and forms water vapour. It spreads out through the air. The air is full of tiny particles of dust. High in the air these dust particles are cold. When water vapour reaches the particles, it condenses on their surfaces and forms tiny water droplets. Billions of droplets form at once and make a cloud. The wind blows the clouds away.

FREEZING

When the clouds are blown into a colder region, such as the air over a hilltop, the droplets at the top of the cloud freeze. They turn to ice crystals which join together and form snowflakes.

The air lower in the cloud is warmer than the air at the top. As the snowflakes fall through the cloud, they melt and turn into large drops of water. The clouds look dark and threatening.

RAIN
The large drops are too heavy to stay in the cloud and fall as rain.

OVER THE GROUND
The rainwater flows away in streams and rivers back to the lakes and seas.

FROM THE GROUND TO THE AIR
Rainwater soaks into the soil and is taken up by plant roots. Most of the water passes through the plant and escapes through the leaves as water vapour.

A diagram of the water cycle.
1 The water evaporates. 2 Clouds form. 3 The water in the clouds freezes. 4 The water falls as rain. 5 Plants soak up the rainwater. 6 Rainwater flows back to the sea. The process begins again.

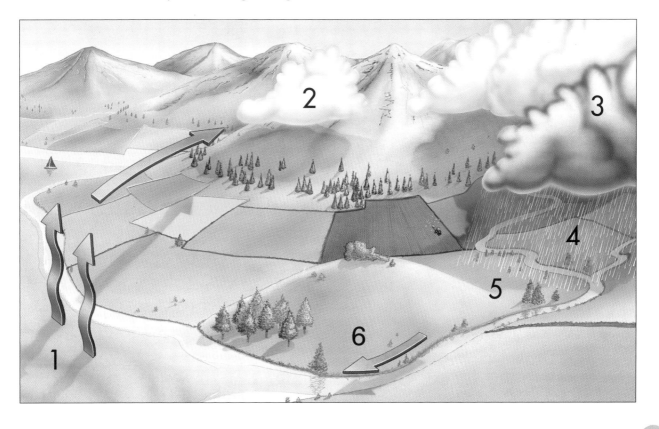

MIXING

Different materials can be mixed together. The mixture formed may have different properties from the materials it is made from.

MIXING SOLIDS AND LIQUIDS

Dry clay is made from tiny particles that you can see. Water is made from very tiny particles you cannot see. When the clay and water are mixed the clay particles separate and spread out between the water particles. The two materials form a new material which can hold a shape.

This clay and water mixture is being shaped into a vase.

DISSOLVING

Sugar and salt are materials that dissolve in water. When a material dissolves it splits up into very tiny particles you cannot see. The particles spread out between the water particles and make the salt or sugar seem to disappear.

The sugar in this spoon dissolves as soon as it touches the water.

THE AIR WE BREATHE

Air is a mixture of gases. One of the gases in the mixture is oxygen. We take this gas from the air when we breathe in and use it to stay alive.

Gases from car engines mix with the air. Some of these gases are harmful. If they occur in large amounts in the air, they cause air pollution which can damage people's health.

When car and truck engines are working they burn fuel and make gases which pass down an exhaust pipe and into the air.

MATERIALS THAT DON'T MIX

Some materials appear to mix at first but separate later. When particles of soil are mixed with water in a jar they form a cloudy suspension. This means that the soil particles are just hanging in the water. In time the particles settle to the bottom of the jar and form a sediment.

■ INVESTIGATE!

Stir some oil and water together Can you get them to mix?

The suspension of soil in the water (left) soon settles out into a sediment at the bottom of the jar (right).

SEPARATING MATERIALS

Some materials that have been mixed together can be separated again later. Sieving and filtering can be used to separate particles of different sizes. Evaporating can be used to separate water from the materials dissolved in it.

SIEVING

A sieve can be used to separate a mixture of two solid materials which have particles of different sizes. There are holes in a sieve. Material particles that are larger than the holes stay in the sieve. Material particles that are smaller than the holes pass through the sieve.

FILTERING

A mixture of a liquid and a solid that does not dissolve can be separated using a very fine sieve called a filter. Most filters are made of paper that has tiny holes in it. The liquid can squeeze through the holes but the solid cannot.

The filter that this cyclist is wearing separates the dust out of the mixture of air and dust that he is breathing.

EVAPORATION

A solid which has been dissolved in water can be separated from the water by evaporation. If the mixture is poured into a dish, the water evaporates. When it does this, the water particles escape into the air and form water vapour. The solid particles cannot do this and are left behind in the dish.

DISTILLATION

Ink is a mixture of water and dissolved colour particles. They can be separated by heating and cooling. The ink is heated in the flask and the water turns to steam. The steam passes along the pipe and cools down. It condenses to water in the pipe which drips out into the beaker.

INVESTIGATE!

Sieve some wholemeal flour to make some white flour.

Steam rises from the heated ink. It travels down the pipe.

Cold water flows around the pipe to keep it cool so that the steam condenses into water.

Ink

Water

REVERSIBLE CHANGES

Separating materials is the opposite or the reverse of mixing them. Separating is a reversible change. Mixing is sometimes a reversible change.

PERMANENT CHANGES

Some processes cannot be reversed. They are called non-reversible, or permanent, changes. Mixing is sometimes a non-reversible change. Non-reversible changes can also take place when materials and mixtures are heated.

BAKING BREAD

Some bread is made from flour, water, yeast and sugar. These four ingredients are mixed together to make dough. Yeast is a type of a fungus. It feeds on sugar.

The ingredients for making bread.

This lump of dough is warming in a bread tin whilst the yeast feeds. After baking it will become a loaf.

When the dough is warmed the yeast feeds quickly and grows. As it feeds the yeast makes carbon dioxide gas. This forms bubbles in the dough and makes it rise. When the dough is baked the yeast is destroyed, the flour is made digestible and the bubbles in the dough expand and make it spongy. The change from dough to bread cannot be reversed.

BURNING

When some materials get hot they burst into flame and burn. They produce the gas carbon dioxide which escapes into the air. A material called ash is left behind. The black colour in ash is carbon that has not changed to carbon dioxide. The rest of the ash is made from other substances that were in the material. Burning is a non-reversible reaction.

Ash is left behind as wood burns on an open fire.

FIRING

When clay is heated strongly, its particles stick together to make a hard, brittle material that is used for pottery and bricks. This process is called firing.

INVESTIGATE!

Examine some food before it is cooked and make notes about its properties. Examine the food after it has been cooked. Discover how its properties have changed.

NEW MATERIALS

The world is full of natural materials such as wood and stone that we can use. By mixing and heating natural materials we can make new materials with new properties.

Liquid steel is poured into a mould which shapes the metal when it cools down.

MIXING METALS

Iron is a natural metal. It is strong but brittle. If iron is melted and oxygen is blown through the liquid iron, steel is made. Steel is also strong, but not brittle. Steel is used to make wire, cans and car bodies. Steel rusts when it gets damp. If it is mixed with the metals nickel and chromium, stainless steel is made which does not rust. It can be used to make kitchen sinks and cutlery.

The steel in these scrapped cars is about to be recycled. It may be made into scissors or paper clips next time.

Light-weight and heat-resistant materials are needed to build rockets for space craft.

KEEPING DRY

Many scientists work at making new materials. The materials have properties which are helpful in special ways. Gore-Tex is an example of a new material which allows sweat to escape from a jacket without rain water soaking in. It allows people to feel more comfortable when they are hiking or climbing.

This picture shows a close up of the fabric Gore-Tex. It is made from a combination of materials.

MATERIALS IN SPACE

New materials have allowed us to explore space. Cermets are materials made from metals and ceramics. They do not break up when they get hot and are used in making rockets.

■ INVESTIGATE!

Make lists of the natural and manufactured materials you use. Which list is longer?

GLOSSARY

ABSORBENT – a property of a solid material which has tiny spaces in it. The solid can take up a liquid into the spaces. Some solids can also take up gases and are used to remove smells such as those of sweaty feet in shoes.

ASH – a grey-black powder which is a mixture of substances from a material that has been burnt.

BOILER – a metal tank which is kept full of water and is heated to provide hot water for a home.

CEMENT – a grey substance used to stick bricks together. It is made from clay and limestone which have been heated together then made into a powder and mixed with water.

CERAMIC – a material made of baked clay.

COMBINATION – a collection. A material is said to have a combination of properties when it has a number of properties, such as soft, flexible and transparent. If an object is made from a collection of materials such as fabric, wood, glue and nails in a sofa, it is said to be made from a combination of materials.

CONCRETE – a hard substance made by mixing sand, cement, small pieces of rock and water together. It is used for making paths, foundations to houses, and the supports in tall buildings and bridges.

CONDUCTOR – a material such as a metal which lets heat or electricity pass though it.

CRYSTAL – a solid material with flat sides arranged at angles to each other. Table salt is a common crystal.

DISTILLATION – a process of separating a solid and a liquid by heating and cooling. The solid is dissolved in the liquid and makes a solution. This is heated and the liquid turns into a gas leaving the dissolved substance behind as a solid. The gas is then cooled away from the solid and turns back into a liquid.

FABRIC – a material made from threads of wool, cotton, nylon or other kinds of fibres. The threads are woven or knitted together to make a piece of cloth.

FILTER – a material such as paper or cloth which is used to separate very small solid particles from liquids and gases.

FLEXIBLE – a property of a material which allows it to be bent without breaking.

FROST – water vapour which has condensed on the ground or on windows then has frozen.

GLASS – a hard, brittle, usually transparent substance which is made by heating sand very strongly with limestone and a chemical called soda.

ICICLE – a long thin pointed piece of ice which hangs down usually from a roof. It forms when dripping water freezes.

INSULATOR – a material, such as thick wool, that does not let heat pass through it, or a material such as pottery or wood which does not let electricity pass through it.

LEAD – a plastic coated wire which is used to carry electricity. A lead usually has a plug at both ends. One end will be plugged into a piece of equipment and the other end into a supply of electricity.

OPAQUE – a property of a material, such as stone, which prevents light from passing through it.

RADIATOR – a piece of equipment which gives out heat to warm up a room. It may be filled with hot water from a boiler. The water's heat is lost into the room.

RECYCLE – a process in which a material such as metal, glass or plastic is used again. The process begins by separating the material from rubbish then sending it to a factory where it is cleaned, melted and made into a new object.

RIGID – a property of a material which prevents the material from being bent, squashed or stretched.

ROCKET – a type of engine on a space craft. Fuel is burnt in it to produce a force which moves the space craft. Large rocket engines are used to launch spacecraft. Small rocket engines are used to steer space craft in space.

ROCKWOOL – a material made from fine fibres. The fibres are made by melting rock and blowing steam through it.

SEDIMENT – a layer of solid particles which forms at the bottom of a container holding a liquid. The particles do not dissolve in the liquid but mix with it when the liquid is stirred. Once the liquid stops moving the particles sink and form the sediment.

SIEVE – a piece of equipment with holes in it or made from wire netting. A sieve is used for separating solid particles of different sizes such as sand and small stones.

SOLVENT – a liquid which can dissolve other substances in it. Water is a solvent. It can dissolve solids like a sugar and gases like carbon dioxide to make fizzy drinks.

STEEL – a metal made from iron. There are different kinds of steel. They are used for making food cans, car bodies, saws and the metal structure of new houses.

SYRUP – a liquid made by dissolving sugar in boiling water. It is used to make sweets.

TEMPERATURE – a measure of the hotness or coldness of a substance. It is measured by using a scale on a thermometer.

TRANSPARENT – a property of a material, such as glass or water, which lets light pass through it.

VOLUME – the amount of space which is taken up by a material. The volume of a block of wood is found by measuring its length, width and height and multiplying the measurements together.

INDEX